Glare

poems by

Gabriella T. Rieger

Finishing Line Press
Georgetown, Kentucky

Glare

ACKNOWLEDGMENTS

With gratitude to my professors at Bar-Ilan University, especially Marcela
Sulak, and to my classmates Jillian Jones and Joanna Chen.

With thanks to my teachers at the Bowery Poetry Club: Bob Holman, Kristin
Prevallet, and Brenda Coultas, who grounded me in an Applied Poetics.

Previously published work:

Binate (*Sanctuary Anthology*, Darkhouse Books)
Mourning as a Carrier Woman (*Yew*)
Solastalgia (*Sanctuary Anthology*, Darkhouse Books)
The Bearer (*The Ilanot Review*)
The EMTs (*The Ilanot Review*)
Witness (*Yew*)

Publisher: Leah Maines
Editor: Christen Kincaid
Cover Art: Daniella Santoro
Author Photo: Daniella Santoro
Cover Design: Elizabeth Maines McCleavy

Printed in the USA on acid-free paper.
Order online: www.finishinglinepress.com
also available on amazon.com

Author inquiries and mail orders:
Finishing Line Press
P. O. Box 1626
Georgetown, Kentucky 40324
U. S. A.

Table of Contents

For my father,
whose appreciation for the written word
and the human heart were a north star

Part I

"So I'll continue to continue to pretend
My life will never end
And flowers never bend
With the rainfall"

—Simon & Garfunkel

The Wishbone

The bird's furcula connects clavicles for flight
the downward swoop and upward stroke.
Freeing bone from connective tissue
bears a wish, or two
with fingered strength in unison,
and an even break.

But that first night, an uncommon visitor,
a wince worn by the angel of reality
While my body before marble
stillness, silently hopes
do not be underwhelmed, be overtaken.

With you there is only restraint, even
in early morning,
nestled spine to chest

(unlike those who would plough through,
breaking my body in two
as a chicken cracked mid-breast).

Your pointed nose and long bones carry well,
a soliloquy, silently under their own spell.
But once, I saw it there, (the wish we might make)
on the edge of Little Italy's ebullient,
narrow streets.

Atop the tenement stone steps, bowing,
under the weight of a century's hurried feet
before the sun hurled us into the hum
of day.

Those hours of life's anatomy laid bare
the urge to consume
each other's history.

And then, the uncommon angel.

You hesitate and bow your head
pull back in on your intact
ribcage,
your unusual, quiet heart
your solemn mouth.

leaving me in the foreground
in the open space I try to fill,
when I recall that night at 3am, I found your wishbone.
I covet it, still.

A hand on either side,
fingers poised for the uneven break,
the angel's wince,
the uncracked flesh, the wishbone
in your breast.

Mourning as a Carrier woman

A widow carried her husband's bones
On her back for a year
Through the nomadic grasses of Canada
I traced the city streets in your absence

On her back for a year
In that room full of windows and wide planks of wood
In my mind, I traced the city streets in your absence
Home became a place to pass through

In that room full of windows and wide planks of wood
I prepared to rip my clothes
Home became a place to pass through
So where would I put your bones, when it came to that

I prepared to rip my clothes
There was no one left to consult
So where would I put your bones, when it came to that
I couldn't trace your steps on the pavement

There was no one left to consult
The dogs rose, circled, slumped back down
I couldn't trace your steps on the pavement
I waited for you, through the second day

The dogs rose, circled, slumped back down
What language would I use in mourning
I waited for you, through the second day
In Budapest or New York or Boston

What language would I use in mourning
Through the nomadic grasses of Canada
Or Budapest or New York or Boston
A widow carried her husband's bones

Passages

Wandering the underbelly of Lincoln Center
ascending to the firefly chandeliers of the Met
texting the boys of my early childhood
the boys of tag, teasing, and racing to the corner mailbox and back again

I forget momentarily how the doctor said, for women of young middle age
and the questions doled out
any children. none.
any pregnancies. one.
Without a vaginal birth, the cervix may not open
The examination room his opera
and this explanation, his aria
It is a potential opening,
like your mouth when your lips part and take in air

It becomes a dance—
the speculum, a slight tug with the tenaculum
the catheter, the balloon, the saline, the wand
and then he said, *I will now restore the dignity,*
I took from you.

An age inspired by a Wim Wenders film, one of the dark, slow
ones that hovers in the air, like the scent of Jasmine competing with
    sunlight.
or the meditations of a Paolo Sorrentino,
yes, I suppose this is young middle age, to sit alone at the Met.

and smile when the eight year old behind you is overcome
by bold leaps of orange and yellow and glittering feathers.
or to watch the fountain rise and fall as it has so many times and
    simultaneously recall
when it was an abyss of construction and tepid waiting,

and too when it was an immovable figure.
only to find yourself, here again, still delighted by the leaps of light
    breathing in the water, as it rises on command.

To descend the subway stairs and know the steps
like old friends. To settle into an acceptance,
it will never be a slight approximation of what it was or should have
    been.
instead, it will continue to be harder and easier in unison.
it will rise and fall as the water in the fountain and the Golden Cockerel
    on stage
it recedes in circadian rhythms, as the ocean I conjure while the
    doctor and technician, maneuver in tandem, take 3D images of the
    uterine wall.
A uterus of young middle age, a Manhattan dusk.

The subway pulls into the station as it has everyday since you got your
    sea legs,
gripping the pole, stumbling as it sped
and too, as you experienced it with your best friend on the 2 train,
in the moment before full adolescence.
Have you ridden the express before? You can float.
He encourages you to raise your arms to the level of your shoulders,
    feel the speed and the track move you
as it has always, and as if for the first time,
New York, the speed, the sway.

Young middle age, nodding to a dune buggy, to Frank O'hara,
thinking, maybe 40 is enough.
The sadness imbued, as the years pass in those black and white images.

It is common for women of young middle age
a song of being.

Solastalgia

Solastalgia (n): "A condition described by the philosopher Glenn Albrecht as a kind of existential grief for a vanished landscape, be it a swallowed coast, a field turned to desert, or a bygone geological epoch." —Ross Andersen

Grandmother Cell: an antiquated theory of cognition that supposed the memory of a person, place, or event was held in a single cell, e.g., the memory of your grandmother.

I thought I left you tucked away in a grandmother cell,
but that too is a myth of cognition.

Remember when we went to hear Franz Wright
at the Jamaica Plain Cemetery—it was perfect

except for the poetry. Paul's mother died
I wanted to tell you,

but you were too far, our conversations of late too few.
The other day, on the phone, I was more New York than you could
     bear.

I wanted to let you fall away, except
who would remember the horizon

of our imperfect excursions,
the contours of our partings,

the visions of tractors and subways—your voice
is familiar, distant; a destabilizing juxtaposition.

The Italian restaurant on La Salle is still there. And with it,
the angles of your frame through my camera lens.

And saying goodbye to our goodbyes.
And the realization that I had achieved something,

merely by losing you,
because in this abandoned landscape I had lived.

Part II: Resonant

Binate

Binate (adj., botany): produced or borne in pairs

It is as if the train will forever sit in Lod
and never move on to Tel Aviv and the great cypress trees of the North,
to Caesarea at the edge of the sea,
to the Baha'i Temple, an arc to desert floras.

I've been wandering this teaming oasis for awhile now,
watching the bedrock of shifting borders sprouting checkpoints,
grey concrete slabs laid in one by one.
I can see the winnowing away of East Jerusalem from the ramparts,
Ma'arat HaMachpela partitioned and barred in cast iron.

Here in this land where every place has two names
I am one of many
I help the wheel turn without knowing direction.
On the road to the Dheisha refugee camp, homes of Martyrs once
     stood,
now children gather scrap metal in shopping carts.

I still dream of olive trees, Yousef,
I plant them for you here,
in Palestine.
This is what American Jews do, we plant trees in Eretz Yisrael
and dedicate them to our grandparents.
Our grandparents who survived or did not survive the Holocaust
who sought refuge
who walked the streets with stars sewn to their clothes
who hid, who ran, who crossed the Pyrenees,
who spent three years in a detention camp in Jamaica
who moved boulder by boulder in the Gush irrigating the land

who built universities and hospitals
who thought the Sinai War was the war that would end all wars.
Who closed the streets of Hebron,
the storefronts, for more than 10 years
painted a green line on a cement divider
and directed traffic: Jews to the left, Arabs to the right
HaMachpelah, Al-haram al-ibrahimi, split
the tomb of our ancestors
Jews in one entrance
Arabs another
Al-Khalil, Hebron
Avraham, Ibrahim
the tomb of our forefathers

The Collectors

I
What cannot be taken—
The angular bareness of tree branches in winter.
The grey Hudson, my oldest friend.

We of the second and third generation
try to recreate the loss of everything.
But all we can do is collect—
seashells, children's drawings, tiny painted handprints,
postcards from other continents.

Zaide collected cereal box barcodes
so we could each have spoons with our names on them.
Mine said, *Gabriella did it!*
What did we do
we exist, light candles in the window frame.

II
Zaide came across a book by a fellow survivor, in it
a photograph of school children.
There was no one to ask if it was her
no parents, no siblings, no old friends.

and how was it, the whole galaxy pulled from its struts
what do you want to know?
They all died.

Who did you go to school with in Poland
what were your shoes made from
and who made them
were you really friends with the Catholic Poles
what did your dinner table look like

What do you want to know
they all died

what did you eat for supper
where did you bike to
how far did you walk
what games did you play

you don't want to know

How long were you there?

I could only leave the ground at night
to relieve myself
one of my brothers was with me
it was a hole in the ground under the barn
then he left to take his chances
three years I stayed there
I was a soldier in the Polish Army
until the war
my parents sold cloth
my mother made challah for Shabbat
I had seven brothers and sisters
they all died
I think this is my sister here
but I'm not sure

The Bearer

When I was old enough
I was entrusted with the task of bringing the soup.
The oriental rug spread out before me
a vast and barren field, ending in a window
overlooking rooftops supporting water towers.
I the lone bearer all the way to the dining room.
Each step awkwardly determined
Arms rigid.
The yellow soup edged itself over the inner rim of the bowl
  And back again.
Heat rose in a steam
of chicken, carrots, dill, parsnip, and kneidlach.
A soup that could make one forget
tights loose and slipping all the way to shul
the lack of bedroom furniture and grandfathers

The soup was eaten in a quiet reprieve
unlike the silence before challah
The silver soup spoon awkward and large for my mouth
was hidden in the suitcase
as they drove from Luxembourg to Antwerp
past the border at dawn, while Nazi soldiers waited for orders.
I remember we had left the house
when my mother said wait, some food or something to wet our lips
but it was too late to leave the car
my grandmother brought the silverware from Antwerp
I remember that. You know we were lucky to have a car.

Many years later I stared at the wooden floor
absolutely bare of lint or thread or spot.
I learned there was another carpet
underneath the one I tread on
carrying plates of gifilte fish.
Carrots and onions crowned each slice
surrounded by a small pool of cold broth.

I'd reach over others at the table
without notice, lean around shoulders and elbows.
Past the slow build of arguments, queries
about the article in today's Times
straight to the center of the plate.
A circle inside a circle.
The white tablecloth gleamed under the brass chandelier.
The meal would conclude with a colorful compote
thick and purple or red with rhubarb.

As my grandmother ladled the steamy liquid
my mother added the vegetables
each delicate and flowing in tandem
Each bowl individually assigned as our seats at the table
And careful, it's hot, don't burn yourself, watch the carpet
I watch the yellow liquid sway—
aren't there more years for me to practice
balance, poise, and memory.

Leaving the Garden

My grandmother is fired up,
hands wave in energetic emphasis
Your mother asked you what you wanted—
I remember—at two years old. Two years old!—
What you wanted to eat, to drink, to wear.
Two years old.
She shakes her head, looks at me, then down and away.
She says, looking straight at me,
I told her serve what you have.
You give what you have.

Part III: Dissection

The Marriage of Bodies

a half to rise with the sun
a half to absorb
the constant motion
a half to sleep with the moon
but a gear wears down, loosens

you always needed something to wind up
or down depending
on the circadian rhythms
of thought
and physiology
creaking against each other

a half to absorb
the grinding and constant motion
to wait for the click
and the moment of calm
that balances on the whim
of the body
and Pavlovian chimes
and the sprouting
of last year's seeds

The survival game

He stood tall in the doorframe; wore a smile whose lips had been working on a sales pitch all day long. We were so familiar I almost forgot he was long lost and my name the last on his list. There were no rings on my fingers. He cried on the phone in Phoenix, for money, any amount. My mouth opened on command, I reported the rent. There was a business idea knocking in his head, the last insistent reflex. The camera bag sat waiting for him to get to it. I smiled while my stomach ate itself. A voice and hands went through the motions, aiming the camera at me. They turned the aperture and shutter speed with long fingernails and knew none of these terms, only Oxycontin and Heroin. He said, *take it, it's a Christmas present,* paused and continued, *how 'bout a nickel for everything?* Still needing the $500, the game weaved its way through the evening, an old tune, sung too often, around the quiet body I did not own. He carried the camera bag on his broad defeated shoulder. I weaved through the darkness with him and his spine, tired of the pins holding it together. He danced for the owner of the camera shop, who laughed and said, *can you believe this guy?* The cash was inevitable. The afterimage of his big brother required me to cushion the hardness of the bills. We had dinner in an all-night café, wound up in Central Park just before dawn. Walking home I allowed his confused body to accompany me. I closed the door. His handprint echoed on the wall, in an expanse of white paint.

The EMTs

my God
even the dogs my God even
the dogs my God the dogs the dogs the blood
even the dogs have blood on them even the dogs
have blood on them my God
the dogs

In conversation with the fixtures

I circle the circle of our beginning
and enter the silence again

Grasp onto the sink
live there on the rim
The pipes beckon me

The paint knows
as the floorboards who bend to my back
Violence has no mastermind, only impulse

I try to lift myself out
onto the sunlight
The walls line up to levy it

One plan runs through itself and begins again
like the rain and the sun on the wheat
that is cropped, bundled, and left to be carried away

Survive these hours

Witness

Certain days halve a life.
A pomegranate cracked wide open
on the heap
there are too many songs in me.

Witness can turn one—
the red, the glare you return to
or never turn toward.

There are many ways to lose
one's husband.

Rain wears at the roof, the door jams shut.
Sometimes you need to apply a little elbow grease
that or grace.

Each day begins again
and we must let it—

maroon boots laced in a loop
pants tucked by a rubber band.

The first pawn
you move into a field.

I was carved
a groove for the peaks and valleys of sound
or the scratch.

In Norway it is said
what would we do without the ocean
we'd carry the boats.

Gabriella T. Rieger received her M.A. in Poetry from Bar-Ilan University. In addition, she studied at The Bowery Poetry Club, The Poetry Project, and Naropa's Summer Writing Program. Her work has appeared in *Transmission, Bowery Women, Voices Israel, The Ilanot Review, Yew,* and *Sanctuary*. Her poem, "Binate" was nominated for the Pushcart Prize. A native New Yorker, the five boroughs are her eternal home.